MW01243758

POEM YOUR HEART OUT
PROMPTS, POEMS & ROOM TO ADD YOUR OWN

FROM THE POETIC ASIDES POEM-A-DAY CHALLENGE

VOLUME 1
APRIL 2014

WORDS DANCE PUBLISHING
WordsDance.com

Copyright © Words Dance Publishing 2014

All poems are copyright of their respective creators as indicated herein, and are reproduced here with permission. No part of this book may be used or performed without written consent from the author except for in critical articles & reviews.

1st Edition
ISBN-13: 978-0692317464
ISBN-10: 0692317465

Prompts written by Robert Lee Brewer
Compiled & orchestrated by Robert Lee Brewer

Proofread by Amanda Oaks & Robert Lee Brewer
Cover & interior design by Amanda Oaks

Cover graphic design elements used with permission, credits include:

Tamsin Baker @ TamsinBaker.com
Carrie Stephens @ FishScraps.com
Vivian @ PetitClipart.Etsy.com
OddHearts.DeviantArt.com

Type set in Bergamo & Brush Up

Find the Poetic Asides blog at **WritersDigest.com**

Words Dance Publishing
WordsDance.com

POEM YOUR HEART OUT
PROMPTS, POEMS & ROOM TO ADD YOUR OWN
VOLUME 1 APRIL 2014

This book *is* poetry. Poetry is a paradox. It's hard to define and pin down, and this book was intentionally designed that way as well.

On one hand, this book is an anthology of the best poems written during the 2014 April PAD (Poem-A-Day) Challenge on the Poetic Asides blog. Each day, hundreds of poets from around the world arrived at the blog, took the day's prompt, and wrote their poetic responses in the comments box.

There were days that topped 1,000 comments, and the 30 poems that made it into this book show the quality of work that can rise out of such overwhelming quantity (21,000+ comments total on the month). Each poem had to make it through me to end up in front of a guest judge who made the final decisions for each day.

30 days, 30 guest judges, 30 winning poems. So an enjoyable anthology of poetry on one hand.

On the other hand, this is a book of poetry prompts. Read the winning poems, but take in the writing prompt that inspired the poem. Consider how the winning poem used the prompt. Sometimes, the connection is obvious. Other times, it's less than obvious.

Let both, the prompt and poem, inspire you to take a stand and create your own poetic masterpieces. This brings us to the third hand. Since I've already used both of mine, the third hand will have to be yours, which is fine, because this is also a workbook of sorts. You're encouraged—heck, *dared*—to write your own poems in this book.

Maybe you participated in April and want to document your efforts during the month. Maybe you're starting now, like so many before you, with just a prompt, an example poem, and an invitation to poem your heart out!

—*Robert Lee Brewer*

p.s. Thank you to Amanda Oaks for having the courage to take on this project and make it her own. From the title to the design, thank you so much!

p.p.s. Thanks also to the incredible guest judges who volunteered their time, talent, and enthusiasm to this project. It made all the difference.

DAY 1

PROMPT

BEGINNINGS AND/OR ENDINGS POEM

Guest Judge
Traci Brimhall

1. Write a beginning poem. Today is the beginning of this challenge. But there are so many other beginnings: Beginning of a relationship, beginning of school, beginning of the rest of your life, and so on. Pick a beginning to write about.

2. Write an ending poem. Often, though not always, beginnings come as the result of an ending. Sometimes endings are cause for disappointment, heartbreak, or numbness. Other times, endings are celebrated. Capture an ending today.

CATHEDRA

you will know
the hoof
of satan's
chosen
deer
by the way
it glows
when any
female
announces
from the seat
of a stilled
tractor
that she
is pregnant–

you will be the age
of your mother's
baby bump

older than your father's
knife

and lit
by the grape
in god's
mouth

– Barton Smock

DAY 1 : YOUR POEM

DAY 2

PROMPT

VOYAGE POEM

Guest Judge
Neil Aitken

For today's prompt, write a voyage poem. A voyage can happen in a variety of ways–by car, on foot, or even psychologically. Heck, the process of writing a poem is a sort of voyage all its own.

SEDOKA

thick fog
unfolding and folding
along the country road

what questions
do the family of deer
hold within their mute crossing?

– Stewart C Baker

DAY 2 : YOUR POEM

DAY 3

PROMPT

MESSAGE POEM

Guest Judge
Shaindel Beers

For today's prompt, write a message poem. Messages can be delivered in a variety of ways: postcard, e-mail, text message, letter in a bottle, smoke signals, secret codes, jumbotron proposals, etc. Also, messages themselves can be simple, complicated, nice, mean, happy, sad, and so on. Get at it!

BELLE BOYD, CONFEDERATE SPY, IMAGINES A LETTER FROM HER SHADOW SISTER

Dear sister, what makes a man think he knows
how the world works when about me he knows nothing,
neither body nor soul? On our first night he dared not
look down at me. His hands like a blind man's.
My body like braille he could not read.

Next morning I drew on my riding clothes,
took out my crop and went riding alone,
kicking the mare so hard she reared, cried out.
We tore over John's Creek, then Sullivan's Ridge
where far off I could see Lee's encampment.
Oh, how I longed to be there, my hair cropped
short, no lacy pantaloons tripping
my feet when I ran through
the thickets. I rode my horse hard all the way home,
spit flying like wedding lace back at me.
We shook the peach blossoms
down on our heads, as they surely fell during battle
at Shiloh from so many bullets
that buzzed round those poor martyred men.

I tell you, I would have knelt down beside them
at Bloody Pond, mingling my blood in the water
where they crawled to drink. Here in my husband's
house, I see my blood every month in the basin.
No child in my womb.
There has never yet been any blood
on our marriage bed.
Sister, I am afraid of my passion
as closer the Union troops draw to our fields.
I fear my passion and what it may do to us both.

– Kathryn Stripling Byer

DAY 3 : YOUR POEM

DAY 4

PROMPT

"SINCE (BLANK)" POEM

Guest Judge
Vince Gotera

For today's prompt, take the phrase "Since (blank)," replace the blank with a word or phrase, make the new phrase the title of your poem, and then, write your poem. Possible titles include: "Since the Last Time I Smoked," "Since You Said Please," and "Since When."

SINCE I AM TAKING A BREAK FROM FACEBOOK

I won't know which color I am.
There won't be signs that tell me
which friends like to give
away the ending of movies
and television shows.
I won't feel obligated to like much
of anything 16 times a day.
There won't be that sensation
that I can post what's on my mind
and everyone will appreciate
my point of view.

I won't need to document
everything in text or a trail of photographs.
There will be words to write down
and I will turn them on their sides
so that they become poems
no one ever sees.
I won't accidentally get into
disputes and turn into a dragon.
There will be an almost instantaneous
lack of knowledge of the existence
of bacon and cats.

I will slip out the back with a singular click.
There won't be much
to say since my words will disappear.
I will often wonder what happened
to the Idaho moose or whose
children were most precocious.
There won't be much to say
because I have said it all before
and instead of recycling my own
typing, I will leave them wondering
if I became a suburban legend.

    – *k weber*

24

DAY 4 : YOUR POEM

DAY 5

PROMPT

DISCOVER SOMETHING POEM

Guest Judge
Patricia Fargnoli

For today's prompt, write a discovery poem. The narrator could discover an object, a person, an animal, a dishonorable deed, or any number of things. Poets can focus on the discovery, examine the aftermath, or even just mention it in passing.

HUBRIS

I did not know
anything but that I wanted
to hold his silky
heft in my small hand.
More than a plum,
less than an apple.
I made a scoop
of my palm, fetched
the weeks-old rabbit
from the well
of dirt he huddled
in with five siblings.
Above the burrow,
dandelions buff
with yellow, burned.
His small ears,
skeleton, the fur
against my thumb
the color of pecans.
He shivered and coiled
tight, snail-like
nose to tail. I felt such
joy and named him
April. I held his
quickened heart,
instinctual shudder
against a wind
dipping down below
the sunny day's sixty
degrees.

Before I found him
the next morning
holding the whole night's cold
in his hard frame,
I was boundless:
Spirit and mother,
seven years old
and god.

- Sharon Fagan McDermott

DAY 5 : YOUR POEM

DAY 6

PROMPT

NIGHT POEM

Guest Judge
Andrew Hudgins

For today's prompt, write a night poem. Vampires and werewolves? Cool. Clubbing and saloons? You got it. Lovers together alone? Right. Ex-lovers alone on their own? Sure thing. You figure out your night poem—and, yes, (k)night poems are fine too.

HOW TO LIVE IN THE COUNTRY DARK

toss frogs
into a fire
your father made.

find a woman
who's abandoned herself
to being led
by a stick.

let her blind mongrel
lick your palm.

bury a handful
of gravel
call it
the moon's
grave.

hide in houses
hidden
from road.

make at least one friend
whose night vision
is a glass of milk.

double your body
by walking
drunk.

– Barton Smock

DAY 6 : YOUR POEM

DAY 7

PROMPT

SELF-PORTRAIT POEM

Guest Judge
January Gill O'Neil

For today's prompt, write a self-portrait poem. Pretty straightforward, right? That doesn't mean there's not a lot of room for creativity. Just look at artists and their self-portraits; there's a lot of differences in the self-portraits of Kahlo, Schiele, Dali, Van Gogh, and others–and not just because the artists look different themselves.

SELF-PORTRAIT AS THE STATE OF MINNESOTA

"A poem is a naked person." -Bob Dylan

My arteries are water flowing north
to Hudson Bay, east to the Atlantic.
That river down my trunk goes south

to New Orleans picking up silt.
My right shoulder is arrowhead,
the left a prairie advertising for bees.

Both stapler and sticky note
are my heritage; world's largest
twine ball, bundt pan, too.

Once upon a time I walked on water
where I swam in summer. No wonder
I believe in fishes and loaves.

Wild loon with stop-signal eyes
lets out a tremolo, wail and yodel.
Found naked on a northern lake.

           - Susan J. Erickson

DAY 7 : YOUR POEM

DAY 8

PROMPT

VIOLENT AND/OR PEACEFUL POEM

Guest Judge
Tom C. Hunley

1. Write a violent poem. Could be person on person violence, person on animal, animal on animal, nature on person/animal/nature, and so on (insects, erosion, cosmos, etc.).

2. Write a peaceful poem. I suppose this might be the opposite of a violent poem. But perhaps not.

A TASTE FOR PAIN

I love the wind when he is violent.
I like it when he forces up my dress or
Slaps my face. I am the opposite of a sadist,

Finding pleasure in displays of power and
Being taken without warning
In broad daylight.

When he comes, bending trees,
Moving seas inside me,
Sometimes I find myself crying—

I am a child of water—
Holding back is no option
When I love the way he loves.

- Fatima Hirsi

DAY 8 : YOUR POEM

DAY 9

PROMPT

SHELTER POEM

Guest Judge
Kelli Russell Agodon

For today's prompt, write a shelter poem. Shelter might be a structure like a house, apartment, or hotel. Shelter could be a tent or cardboard box. Shelter could be an umbrella, overpass, cave, or car. Shelter could be a state of mind, part of a money laundering scheme, or any number of interpretations.

SHELTER

Hunker down with me
in the afternoon and pretend
the snow's still caught in the gutters
and the cows won't leave the barn
until the April frost has gone away.
Put your eyes on my sweater
and keep them open, stare at
the distorted cross-hatch
as if it might save you and
ignore the purpling stain
of my tear drops on polyester.
The best shelter, mother told me,
after the ice had melted into her
whiskey and the pill cap was off
and the two or three left rattled
like a toddler toy against her acrylics,
the best shelter is the kind you have
to beg for. So I'll beg for you, baby,
to put your skin against mine
and let's dream about winter until
the clouds run west river
and the cows are ready for slaughter.

       - Cameron Steele

DAY 9 : YOUR POEM

DAY 10

PROMPT

FUTURE POEM

Guest Judge
Nate Pritts

For today's prompt, write a future poem. The future might mean robots and computer chips. The future might mean apocalyptic catastrophes. The future might mean peace and understanding. The future might mean 1,000 years into the future; it might mean tomorrow (or next month).

WHAT COMES

The front travels without regard for us.
It seems to know everything.
First wind makes the trees
creak, pine needles swirl in the current.
Lightning comes close —
Once through a kitchen window,
once in a nearby field.
From the porch it is familiar
as an aunt you haven't seen in a long time.
It brings rain that humbles
the lilacs to the ground, the muddy ruts
we are forced to jump over.

It comes to the kids wading in the river.
It comes to those writing, those cooking,
to the one who says, "Next year
we'll put a fence around the pumpkins."
It pays attention to no one.
It has gotten past Why is this happening ?
Doesn't understand what is said to the stars,
doesn't care about what is remembered,
doesn't believe in endings since everything
begins again somewhere else.
It could be anywhere, it likes forests,
I think, it likes August. If it is doing anything,
it is listening to itself harder and harder.

    - Alana Sherman

DAY 10 : YOUR POEM

DAY 11

PROMPT

MAKE STATEMENT TITLE OF POEM

Guest Judge
Joseph Mills

For today's prompt, make a statement the title of your poem and either respond to or expand upon the title. Some example titles might include: "A Date Which Will Live in Infamy;" "Guns Don't Kill People, I Do;" "This Is Your Brain on Drugs;" "Smile for the Camera," and "Be Kind Rewind." Of course, there's an incredible number of possible titles; pick one and start poeming!

DON'T GO THERE

You said, with that hard look when
I tried to tell you that the house
needed a small repair, that you
should call your mother on her
birthday, that maybe later we
could take a trip to Long Island
to see my sister. Don't go there.
I wondered where we might go,
if not there, if we couldn't risk
quick trips to places that cause
dis-ease, poke into dim corners
that might hide small treasures,
a gold coin, a lost child, an old
song, prizes I've glimpsed
at the edge of my vision,
that vision we had at the start.
I have been down that road,
that one you've told me
not to travel, the one that
might take me to the heart
of the heart I once held in my hands.

– *Carole Cole*

52

DAY 11 : YOUR POEM

DAY 12

PROMPT

CITY POEM

Guest Judge
Victoria Chang

For today's prompt, write a city poem. The poem can take place in a city, can remember the city (in a general sense), be an ode to a specific city, or well, you should know the drill by now. City poem: Write it!

FLESH AND LEATHER

Know a city by its stones, oldest
streets worn to ghost step. Both
flesh and leather marched here. Reign
of sun, rake of rain, flood and drought
a buckle. I remember sideroads

best: shops, apartments with tiny
window gardens. I see shadows
of their blossoms. How the woman with
scissors scattered roses down on
soldiers who looked up laughing. Later
her petals would be barefoot as
slaves. So many sorts

of blood. They say it takes a thousand
years to shine a stone, another hundred
to lay them, make them perfectly
uneven, so that, with a stumble,
the city bends its knee.

– Joanne Clarkson

DAY 12 : YOUR POEM

DAY 13

PROMPT

ANIMAL POEM

Guest Judge
Daniel Nester

For today's prompt, write an animal poem. Pick a specific
animal or write about your animal spirit. Maybe you'll get
tricky and write about mustangs (meaning the car) or jaguars
(meaning the American football team). Maybe you'll do an
acrostic, or even go crazy and write a sestina (crickets).

AN(T)I-MAL(L)

Downtown is a blood-clotted cluster of veins,
where light is pollution and the sky never blue,
every hillside quiet as a grave,
waiting for something, anything to break,
to feel that dampness on the edge of the wind,
memory smothered with a shopping mall.

There's a monster, a wad of cash in its maw,
an arrow in its throat like a bad weather vane
oblivious to the direction of the wind,
everything dying, born to be blue,
comfortable in slate as the storm cloud breaks
turning all young faces into open graves.

Time existed before a clock face engraved,
that presence acting on all surfaces like a maul,
pounding, relentless until they crack and they break
an eventuality that makes individuality vain,
why every bird only seems to sing the blues,
and every wild thing needs a window.

An old watch will eventually need winding,
as the joints of giants are grinding into gravel,
the hottest stars are burning bright blue
so far away their beauty is a ghost mallet
leaving an echo where meaning taps its vein,
bulldozer drivers taking their foot off the brake.

The modern age can't stop to take a break,
to wonder where all the breathable air went,
it would destroy the moon to find a precious vein
and tell children to make their wishes graves.
Behind every parking lot there's a skyscraper mal-
ignance, saying sapphires in the sea keep it blue.

The ice caps melted before the volcano blew,
and the eruption lit the night like an early dawn breaking.

These warnings of repetition fall on ears malformed,
as miles of concrete grow to outnumber the wind,
all earth removed part of an unmarked grave
where falling acid rain whispers the words, "in vain."

The needle in the vein was always full of wind,
without green a malicious shade of deoxygenated blue,
a promise that the grave could never break.

– Jay Sizemore

DAY 13 : YOUR POEM

DAY 13 : YOUR POEM

DAY 14

PROMPT

"IF I WERE (BLANK)" POEM

Guest Judge
Jericho Brown

For today's prompt, take the phrase "If I Were (blank)," replace the blank with a word or phrase, make the new phrase the title of your poem, and then, write the poem. Possible titles might include: "If I Were President," "If I Were Smarter," "If I Were a Little More Sensitive," or "If I Were Born on April 14." If I were you, I'd get poeming about now.

IF I WERE YOUR ANSWER

I'd breathe each doubt on
your lips until they were
lost in my lungs. If I were

your answer, I'd fold the
questions on your tongue
into shapes like origami;

a ship, a cloud, a flower,
and with each whispered
kiss I'd blow them away.

I have hidden all of your
unknowns; tucked away
like honeycombs for you

to find— the sweetest
answers are the ones you
have yet to unearth, in me.

– Lori DeSanti

DAY 14 : YOUR POEM

DAY 15

PROMPT

LOVE AND/OR ANTI-LOVE POEM

Guest Judge
Barbara Hamby

1. Write a love poem. Love, it's such a big 4-letter word that can mean so much to so many for a variety of interpretations. Friendly love, sexual love, dorky love, all-encompassing love, jealous love, anxious love, love beaten with a baseball bat, hot love, big love, blues love, greeting card love, forgiving love, greedy love, love in a music video, and so on and so forth.

2. Write an anti-love poem. Well, kinda like love, but take it back the other way.

ROMANTICS

It's not some gilt-edged bound-in-leather journal
in which I write with fancy flourishes,
my quill pen scratching odes to love eternal.

My Bic pen scrawls, its blue ink nourishes
lined paper bound by wire spiral spine,
torn cardboard covers held against their wishes

by duct tape, just to lend a silver shine.
What matters is what's put between the covers,
not whether your book's prettier than mine.

Let's read our work to our respective lovers
and see who swoons to each impassioned page,
and like the tiny hummingbird who hovers

around the nectar jar, their love will rage.
It's so much better than a living wage.

– Bruce Niedt

DAY 15 : YOUR POEM

DAY 16

PROMPT

ELEGY

Guest Judge
Bob Hicok

For today's prompt, write an elegy. An elegy doesn't have specific formal rules. Rather, it's a poem for someone who has died. In fact, elegies are defined as "love poems for the dead" in John Drury's *The Poetry Dictionary*. Of course, we're all poets here, which means everything can be bent. So yes, it's perfectly fine if you take this another direction–for instance, I once wrote an elegy for card catalogs. Have at it!

GRATITUDE

The midmorning suicides are referred to as "incidents"
holding up trains, and the inverse function of distance
is love; or, humanity. Care for one's fellow man (or
woman), who threw everything under the sledgehammer,
increases the closer one is to the scene of the action.
Morning commutes are ordinarily dull: such passion
deserves mention. A bow of the head; a bend in the sound.
Figures in jumpers with shovels and brooms come round
gathering blood and meat, and they, my fellow passengers,
pray it was quick, and clean, that he was a bachelor
with no one to receive this news. In the becalmed car,
fans whir and nobody speaks. Train-turned-church is our
impromptu gift to the dead, who perhaps did not expect
our rediscovered lives to spring red from his neck—
but it does. We test each other's pulse, riding to Shady Grove.
We step out and see the day. The inverse of distance is love.

– Joseph Harker

DAY 16 : YOUR POEM

DAY 17

PROMPT

POP CULTURE POEM

Guest Judge
Mary Biddinger

For today's prompt, write a pop culture poem. Write a poem about Bon Jovi or Van Halen; write a poem about the Kardashians (or don't–and say you did); write a poem about a popular SNL skit; write a poem about *Dr. Who* or *Downton Abbey*; write a poem about any kind of popular culture thing-a-ma-bob you wish. In fact, write three! (Just kidding; you only need to write one poem–but seriously, write three and be sure to add a little more cowbell.)

LESS THAN 120 MINUTES OF ALTERNATIVE

It took some time for me to figure
out that the Seether was Louise,
that Feed The Tree meant dying.
I still don't know who Ezra is.
The Pixies' gigantic, big, big love
ended up spawning a cannonball,
and no one is cooler than Kim Deal,
though it was sad when they went
silent after her twin sister went
into rehab. I never thought she'd
be a junkie because heroin is so
passe. To this day, I'm only happy
when it rains and naturally lonely
and dreaming of the west coast.
There's more to say, but you just
don't get it, you keep it copacetic.
At this point, I have nothing to
offer but confusion and the circus
in my head in the middle of the bed,
in the middle of the night. You
probably don't get that, but I knew
what Kristin was talking about.
I'm just happy I found a girl who
thinks really deep thoughts,
especially when I'm thinking about
sex and candy. Well, I'd better get
out of here. I think the roof is
on fire, but I'm going to let the
motherfucker burn. Burn motherfucker,
burn.

– Kendall A. Bell

DAY 17 : YOUR POEM

DAY 18

PROMPT

WEATHER POEM

Guest Judge
Nin Andrews

For today's prompt, write a weather poem. A weather poem can be a poem about a hurricane or tornado; it can be a poem about the weatherperson; it can be a poem about forgetting an umbrella on a rainy day; it can be big; it can be small; etc.

COLLAPSE

how
on a clear day
my father
is the face
of absence.

how what I mean
cuts the finger
my mother
sips.

how porch blood
is not the same blood
the body
faints with.

how copperhead, how rattlesnake, how lisp

says I myth
my sister
who is still

vanishing
to shoplift
god

from the thunderstorm
we gave her.

- Barton Smock

DAY 18 : YOUR POEM

DAY 19

PROMPT

PICK COLOR, MAKE TITLE OF POEM

Guest Judge
Thomas Lux

For today's prompt, pick a color, make the color the title of your poem, and then, write your poem. You can make your poem black, white, red, purple, turquoise, puce, or whatever your heart desires. And the subject of your poem can cover any topic–as long as you've plugged a color into the title. Let's do this!

AUBERGINE

You are that moment
of twilight on the mountain,
erupting into night—
or the tapestry
on which a field of galaxies
swirl and collide—
the sash draped
across a monarch's throne—
the velvet petal
of a rare orchid blooming
in a remote Oriental garden.

But mostly you are violet,
imbued with earth
and tasting of regret.

– Sara Diane Doyle

DAY 19 : YOUR POEM

DAY 20

PROMPT

FAMILY POEM

Guest Judge
Scott Owens

For today's prompt, write a family poem but you don't have to restrict yourself to your own family. There are any number of human families, of course, but also animals, insects, and other organisms. Plus, there are "families" of other types as well. As usual, feel free to bend the prompt to your favor.

I DRAW A MOUNTAIN

I draw a mountain on a piece of paper,
a small tree, a creek, a little bird and
warily place my family there.
I have hidden my dad in the crab grass
next to the base of the mountain to cover
the sprawling roots of the wavering trees.
My mom is a fluttery mockingbird
imitating life from the treetops and my brother
is the hiker on the mountainside, two
poles on either side for balance, digging,
handling, touching everything with bare hands,
while I float along in current of the creek,
my head bobbing just barely above the water.

   – Brie Huling

DAY 20 : YOUR POEM

DAY 21

PROMPT

BACK TO BASICS POEM

Guest Judge
Deborah Ager

For today's prompt, write a "back to basics" poem. For me, back to the basics means jumping to the fundamentals. Maybe it's me re-learning (or practicing) fundamentals–like running or writing–but it could also be a child learning how to tie his shoestrings, which can be a unique experience for both the child and the adult trying to give instructions and advice. Back to basics could also be re-setting a state of mind or getting back into a routine. In a way, spring is a season that gets back to the basics.

SQUARE ONE

When I am finally ready to admit I don't know how it will end, I go back to the beginning: The moon, bone white and beaten still in an inky sky. You, hands open as though you are trying to catch something that's falling. A star, perhaps. Or me, teetering on the edge of loneliness, sanity, that tiny shivered sliver of gold up there in all that black. Looking back, I think I thought you were Orion himself, some warrior in waiting. And I, a damsel damned and destined to be broken open. Have I not spilled my whole self for you just yet? Let me offer you these last pieces, the shatterings of one unsaved. I craved that sky. And you were just a hunter longing for something to capture, conquer, own.

Me, Love?
I just wanted to be known.

– De Jackson

DAY 21 : YOUR POEM

DAY 22

PROMPT

OPTIMISTIC AND/OR PESSIMISTIC POEM

Guest Judge
Lawrence Schimel

1. Write an optimistic poem. The glass is half full.

2. Write a pessimistic poem. The glass is half empty.

EXPECTATION

He never leaves the house
without latching an umbrella
over his arm—
it swings there, lulling
to the rhythm
of his stride.
Every day, no matter
what the weatherman
predicts.

Most shake their heads,
say what a shame
to always expect
the worst.

But he is no doomsday
prophet—oh no.
He hopes
the mere presence
of the umbrella
will bring on
the storms he so loves
to dance in.

- Sara Diane Doyle

DAY 22 : YOUR POEM

DAY 23

PROMPT

LOCATION POEM

Guest Judge
Erika Meitner

For today's prompt, write a location poem. Location could be physical–like the laundromat, a public park, a glacier, flying saucer, etc. Or location could be emotional, psychological, metaphysical, or some other kind of word that ends in -al. Or surprise everyone!

FIELD OF HOUSES

Our house was burning.
It was in a forest
of blazing homes. No one
in them could sense flames.
Mom kept trying to balance
her checkbook. Dad wanted
his uniforms washed.
My brother and I tried
to invent a new board game,
surviving the apocalypse,
rolling to avoid zombies,
to evade destruction.
Our roofs lit up the night.
Helicopters above them
didn't see the light. Nobody
realized their flesh, charred,
was falling off their bones.
Or that when we waved
to each other we fanned
the sparks in our hair.
I'm sure everyone everywhere
kept doing their daily tasks.
That time was ignored.
I watched the inferno
continue to spread.
The field of houses
were infinite. The heat
would turn us into ashes.
I tried to pretend
I wasn't cooked meat.
That I had a location,
that it wasn't the air.

– Donald Illich

DAY 23 : YOUR POEM

DAY 24

PROMPT

"TELL IT TO THE (BLANK)" POEM

Guest Judge
Kristina Marie Darling

For today's prompt, take the phrase "Tell It to the (blank)," replace the blank with a word or phrase, make the new phrase the title of your poem, and then, write the poem. Possible titles include: "Tell It to the Hand," "Tell It to the Judge," "Tell It to the Six-Foot Bunny Rabbit," and so on.

TELL IT TO MY BROTHER

a widow
with three hands
has ten
doomed
acquaintances.

god's tacklebox is too light
to carry.

think of it as your ascent into feminine indifference.

think of your son as the incurable
made
thing

on the factory floor
of my son's
use.

a male mime
bites into
a bar of soap...

sex
is a bruise
in a blizzard

  – *Barton Smock*

DAY 24 : YOUR POEM

DAY 25

PROMPT

THE LAST STRAW POEM

Guest Judge
Erica Wright

For today's prompt, write a "last straw" poem. Everyone encounters situations in which they decide they're not going to take it anymore (whatever "it" happens to be). It could be a loud noise, an abusive partner, someone taking the Pop Tart but not throwing the box away, or whatever. Write about the moment, the aftermath, or take an unexpected path to your poem.

LAST STRAW

Scarecrow didn't winter well. One last stalk
whispers up his left sleeve. The ragged
plaid shirt hangs on him like sickness. His burlap
face watches field dust more than
sky. It's time to re-seed. Clouds know it
and the crows know it. Time to fill those furrows
with new green. The scarecrow's hunger
is for purpose more than grain. Spring
is difficult for old men, old
women. Today or tomorrow the field hand
will hoist him from these acres
to make way for the plow. He will lie
in his heap of broom stick bones
until someone decides which bits are worth
cobbling into this summer's sentinel.
Young wind sifts chaff from a torn
cuff. Even broken, his shoulders feel
the grip of tiny sparrows.

– Joanne M. Clarkson

DAY 25 : YOUR POEM

DAY 26

PROMPT

WATER POEM

Guest Judge
Amy King

For today's prompt, write a water poem. Life depends upon water, so there are any number of ways to write this prompt. A few thoughts that jump to mind include pollution, rising water levels, hurricanes, fracking, and more.

FAIR ENOUGH

Fill me up
at the clown's mouth
until this shot
breaks my balloon
and you find the prize
is on the inside

Throw another
ball at my red target
and aim for the middle
where the alarms sound
then I fall and struggle
to swim my clothed self

in your glass of water

– k weber

DAY 26 : YOUR POEM

DAY 27

PROMPT

MONSTER POEM

Guest Judge
Jeannine Hall Gailey

For today's prompt, write a monster poem. There are the usual suspects: zombies, vampires, werewolves, and mummies. But monsters can take any form and terrorize a variety of victims. So have fun playing around with this one, because we've only got a few days left.

FORGIVE US OUR DEMONS

skin all your whitman books with butterknives and
patch up my skin, because if my trembling mouth
is a shotgun barrel then we're all in danger, darling,
and the trigger catches up with me some nights

when my brittle teeth draw blood. we were all just
razorblades and bits of broken mirror back then.
you scratched out jagged poetry with the shards,
too afraid to tell me the truth, and we pretended

the monsters had made their homes in our veins
instead of in our heads and we fought back at them
with blood and bruises, the only way we knew how.

sometimes hope is a poison. sometimes freedom
is a noose, and nobody knows that better than us,
do they, darling? I only hope you can forgive me

for not being able to stitch up your scars as well as
mine. I barely have enough thread to keep my own
monsters from creeping back inside, let alone yours.

– Emma Travis

DAY 27 : YOUR POEM

DAY 28

PROMPT

SETTLED POEM

Guest Judge
Sandra Beasley

For today's prompt, write a settled poem. Settled can be a good, relaxing thing; settled can be an accepting something that wasn't your first choice thing; settled can be coming to a stop; settled can be pioneers in a strange land; and so on. With only three days left, don't settle for less than your best.

TRIPTYCH: CONVERSATIONS WITH MY MOTHER

i. October, many years ago

My mother believes that I am the moon,
asks whether this weakness for boys might
just be a phase. Everything is temporary:
celestial bodies, young love, small tears
collecting on the steps of her eyes.
We are talking about two different things.
Listen, I've always been this way, and
I grew tired of hiding: my crescent begins
showing its colors. Daughters-in-law
evaporate one by one in my mother's head.
My mother believes in guiding the lost,
the persistence of heaven, truth in love
no matter the cost. She sits and watches me
open up new sails, lift anchors, cast off.

ii. June, some time later

My mother presses my shirt for a wedding
I'll attend tomorrow with my boyfriend.
She wants to know about the Pennsylvania farm
where it'll be held, the B&B where we'll stay,
the happy couple. What do you want from
me? I invent a few details and crack some joke
about catching the bouquet– but I never know
how to feel about the boys on my surface.
My mother is ranked a grandmaster in hope.
I can see her see my future unfold like origami:
civil unions, adoptions, a minimum of distance.
I'm not ready; I'm only half-done. I tie ropes
round my wrists so I can slip them again. She
adds more water and pushes the iron down.

iii. February, recently

My mother stirs batter as I tell her I'm sick
of being sick of Valentine's Day. Single,
but hopeful, for now. Lately I've been tired
as a forest clearing an hour before dawn:
webbed with dew and ready for a change.
My mother says you meet the right man
when you're ready, and it isn't strange
anymore when she says it. "The right man."
I spent so long hoping you would forget it.
Forty years of marriage means her advice
comes without thinking. Maybe I'm Ulysses
longing for the harbor as much as the moon,
full and ready to wane at last. Maybe she's
the current I've followed so long without sinking.

– Joseph Harker

DAY 28 : YOUR POEM

DAY 28 : YOUR POEM

DAY 29

PROMPT

REALIST AND/OR MAGICAL POEM

Guest Judge
Adam Fitzgerald

1. Write a realism poem. A poem that is rooted in the real world. Or…

2. Write a magical poem. A poem that incorporates magical or fantastical elements.

TRIGGER

Today is a battered guitar crafted
from the light of a new wolf moon
and renewable Canadian cedar.
The strings are made of the glow
of city lights, the rumble of thunder,
the bitterness of coffee, the itch
of poison ivy, the smell of gasoline,
and, well, the sixth string is broken
but it sounded like the dirt under
your porch, Billy, at your house on
birdless Audubon. But with only five
strings, it's more a banjo, jangling
too fast to understand, summoning
cold front clouds and grokking rain
with some minor diminished seventh
chord of gloom, that J-sharp-flat note
JB spent too many late night hours
trying to discover between the notes
of the western scale and the pages of
his misprinted Bible. And so we will walk
all through the night, a thousand miles
and never leave this town, the barbed
hours picking and strumming that old
acoustic guitar in the neon pawn shop
window, the one you swear maybe
once belonged to some old testament
angel or maybe even Willie Nelson.

– James Brush

DAY 30

PROMPT

CALLING IT A DAY POEM

Guest Judge
Jillian Weise

For today's prompt, write a "calling it a day" poem. Some people might call this "Miller time," others may refer to it as "closing time." Just remember: Don't call it a day until you put it in a poem.

AUBADE FOR ALL THINGS RISING, STRONG

It cracks open,
yolk rising along
a sizzled horizon
and we call it
morning and we call it
magic and we call it
magnificent, as colors
braid their way through
dawn's crimson hair.

We collect these fragile gifts into
baskets of seven, christen them
after heavenly bodies,
gods named for our own hunger,
thirst;
call it good.

And the evening
and the morning
were the first.

            – De Jackson

DAY 30 : YOUR POEM

The poems in this book were selected by a wonderful group of guest judges—all very accomplished poets in their own rights. Be sure to check out their work, if you're not familiar with it already.

Deborah Ager recently co-edited *The Bloomsbury Anthology of Contemporary Jewish American Poetry* and *Old Flame: Ten Years of 32 Poems Magazine*. The latter is a finalist for the Forward Book of the Year prize. www.deborahager.com

Kelli Russell Agodon is a poet, writer, and editor from the Northwest. She's the author of *Hourglass Museum* and *The Daily Poet: Day-By-Day Prompts for Your Writing Practice*, co-authored with Martha Silano. Kelli is the co-founder of Two Sylvias Press and was the editor of *Crab Creek Review* for the last six years.

Neil Aitken is the author of *The Lost Country of Sight*, winner of the 2007 Philip Levine Prize, and the editor of *Boxcar Poetry Review*. He was born in Vancouver, British Columbia and raised in Saudi Arabia, Taiwan, and western United States and Canada. www.neil-aitken.com

Nin Andrews' poems and stories have appeared in many literary journals and anthologies, including *Ploughshares*, *The Paris Review*, *Best American Poetry (1997, 2001, 2003, 2013)*, and *Great American Prose Poems*. Her next book, *Why God Is a Woman*, is due out from BOA Editions in 2015.

Sandra Beasley is the author of *I Was the Jukebox, Theories of Falling*, and *Don't Kill the Birthday Girl: Tales From an Allergic Life*, a memoir and cultural history of food allergy. She lives in Washington, D.C., and is on the faculty of the low-residency MFA program at the University of Tampa. www.sandrabeasley.com

Shaindel Beers is the author of two full-length poetry collections, *A Brief History of Time* and *The Children's War and Other Poems*. She's also the poetry editor for *Contrary Magazine*. http://shaindelbeers.com

Mary Biddinger is the author of multiple collections, including *Saint Monica, O Holy Insurgency*, and most recently *A Sunny Place With Adequate Water*. She's also the founder of *Barn Owl Review*. Mary has received two Ohio Arts Council Individual Excellence Awards in Creative Writing for her poetry. www.marybiddinger.com

Traci Brimhall is the author of *Our Lady of the Ruins*, selected by Carolyn Forche for the 2011 Barnard Women Poets Prize, and *Rookery*, winner of the 2009 Crab Orchard Series in Poetry First Book Award. Her poems have appeared in *Poetry*, *The New Yorker*, and *Best American Poetry (2013 and 2014)*. http://tracibrimhall.com

Jericho Brown is the author of *Please*, winner of the 2009 American Book Award, and *The New Testament*. A former speechwriter for the Mayor of New Orleans, Jericho's poetry has been published in several publications, including *The Iowa Review, New England Review,* and *Oxford American*. www.jerichobrown.com

Victoria Chang's third book of poems, *The Boss*, was published by McSweeney's Poetry Series in 2013. Her other books are *Salvinia Molesta* and *Circle*. Her poems have been published in *Kenyon Review, Poetry, American Poetry Review, The Washington Post,* and *Best American Poetry*. www.victoriachangpoet.com

Kristina Marie Darling is the author of 17 books, which include *Melancholia* (An Essay), *Petrarchan*, and *Fortress*. Her awards include fellowships from Yaddo, the Helene Wurlitzer Foundation, and the Hawthornden Castle International Retreat for Writers. http://kristinamariedarling.com

Patricia Fargnoli, from Walpole, NH, was the New Hampshire Poet Laureate from 2006-2009. She's published 4 books (including *Winter* and *Then, Something*) and 3 chapbooks of poetry and has won The May Swenson Book Award, the Foreward Silver Book of the Year Award, and the Sheila Mooton Book Award.

Adam Fitzgerald is the author of *The Late Parade*. He received his MFA from Columbia University's School of the Arts. He is the founding editor of the poetry journal *Maggy* and contributing editor for *The American Reader*. He teaches at The New School and Rutgers University. www.thelateparade.com

Jeannine Hall Gailey recently served as the Poet Laureate of Redmond, WA, and is the author of four books of poetry: *Unexplained Fevers, She Returns to the Floating World, Becoming the Villainess,* and *The Robot Scientist's Daughter* (coming in 2015 from Mayapple Press). www.webbish6.com

Vince Gotera is author of *Fighting Kite*, *Ghost Wars*, and other poetry collections, including the forthcoming *Pacific Crossing*. He also published lit-crit book *Radical Visions: Poetry by Vietnam Veterans*. Vince is the editor of *North American Review* and professor at University of Northern Iowa. http://vincegotera.blogspot.com

Barbara Hamby is the author of five books of poems, including *On the Street of Divine Love: New and Selected Poems*, *Babel*, and *All-Night Lingo Tango*. She won a 2010 Guggenheim fellow in Poetry and her book of short stories, *Lester Higata's 20th Century*, won the 2010 Iowa Short Fiction Award. www.barbarahamby.com

Bob Hicok is the author of several poetry collections, including *This Clumsy Living*, *Animal Soul*, and *Elegy Owed*. He teaches creative writing at Virginia Tech and before teaching owned and ran a successful automotive die design business. His poems have appeared in *Poetry*, *The New Yorker,* and *Best American Poetry*.

Andrew Hudgins is the author of seven books of poems, including *A Clown at Midnight*, *Saints and Strangers*, *The Glass Hammer*, and *Ecstatic in the Poison*. A finalist for the National Book Award and the Pulitzer Prize, he is a recipient of Guggenheim and National Endowment for the Arts fellowships.

Tom C. Hunley is an associate professor of English at Western Kentucky University, the director of Steel Toe Books, and the bassist for the litcore rock band Manley Pointer. Forthcoming are his fourth full-length book, *Plunk*, and an edited collection of essays titled *Creative Writing Studies: An Introduction to Its Pedagogies*.

Of I Want to Make You Safe, John Ashbery describes **Amy King**'s poems as bringing "abstractions of brilliant, jagged life, emerging into rather than out of the busyness of living." *Safe* was one of Boston Globe's Best Poetry Books of 2011. King teaches at SUNY Nassau Community College and works with VIDA: Women in Literary Arts.

Thomas Lux's most recent book of poems is *Child Made of Sand* and *Selected Poems* is due from Bloodaxe Books Fall 2014. Lux holds the Bourne Chair in Poetry and is director of the McEver Visiting Writers Program at the Georgia Institute of Technology. He has been awarded multiple NEA grants.

Erika Meitner's first book, *Inventory at the All-Night Drugstore*, won the 2002 Robert Dana-Anhinga Prize for Poetry. Her second book, *Ideal Cities*, was selected by Paul Guest as a winner of the 2009 National Poetry Series competition. *Copia* (BOA Editions) is due out this year. http://erikameitner.com

A faculty member at the University of North Carolina School of the Arts, **Joseph Mills** holds an endowed chair, the Susan Burress Wall Distinguished Professorship in the Humanities. He has published five collections of poetry with Press 53, including *This Miraculous Turning*. www.josephrobertmills.blogspot.com

Daniel Nester is the author of *How to Be Inappropriate*, *God Save My Queen I and II*, and is editor of *The Incredible Sestina Anthology*. His writing has appeared in *The New York Times*, *The Daily Beast*, and *Best American Poetry*. He teaches writing at The College of Saint Rose in Albany, NY. www.danielnester.com

January Gill O'Neil is the author of *Underlife* and *Misery Islands* (both CavanKerry Press). She is the executive director of the Massachusetts Poetry Festival and an assistant professor of English at Salem State University.

Originally from Greenwood, SC, **Scott Owens** holds degrees from Ohio University, UNC Charlotte, and UNC Greensboro. He currently lives in Hickory, NC, where he teaches at Catawba Valley Community College, edits *Wild Goose Poetry Review*, and serves as vice-president of the NC Poetry Society. www.scottowenspoet.com

Nate Pritts is the author of six books of poetry, including *Right Now More Than Ever*. His poems, and writings about poetry, can be found in *American Poetry Review*, *Southern Poetry Review*, *Poets & Writers*, and *Poet's Market*. He founded H_NGM_N, an online journal and small press. www.h-ngm-n.com/nate-pritts

Lawrence Schimel writes in both English and Spanish and has published over 100 books in many different genres, including the poetry collection *Desayuno en la Cama* (Egales) and the chapbooks *Fairy Tales for Writers* and *Deleted Names*. He has published poems in *The Saturday Evening Post* and *The Christian Science Monitor*.

140

Jillian Weise is the author of *The Amputee's Guide to Sex*, the novel *The Colony*, and *The Book of Goodbyes*, which won the 2013 James Laughlin Award. After fellowships from the University of North Carolina at Greensboro, the Fine Arts Work Center, and the Fulbright Program, she joined the faculty at Clemson University.

Erica Wright is the author of *Instructions for Killing the Jackal* and the chapbook *Silt*. Her debut crime novel, *The Red Chameleon*, was published earlier this year. She is poetry editor at *Guernica Magazine* and has taught at Marymount Manhattan College and New York University's continuing studies program.

Stewart C Baker is a haikuist, speculative fiction author, and academic librarian. Stewart has lived in England, South Carolina, Japan, and California, and now lives in Oregon with his wife and children— although if anyone asks, he'll say he's from the Internet. Find his poetry and fiction online at http://infomancy.net.

Kendall A. Bell's poetry has been widely published in print and online. He is a five time nominee for Best of the Net, has released fifteen chapbooks, is founder and co-editor of the online journal Chantarelle's Notebook and publisher/editor of Maverick Duck Press. His website is www.kendallabell.com.

James Brush lives in Austin, TX, where he teaches high school English. He's the author of *Birds Nobody Loves*, *A Place Without a Postcard*, and many scraps of paper around his house. You can find him online at *Coyote Mercury* (coyotemercury.com), where he keeps a full list of publications.

A native of Georgia, **Kathryn Stripling Byer** lives in the North Carolina mountains. Her six books of poetry (LSU Press, Press 53) have won various awards, including the Laughlin Award from the Academy of American Poets for *Wildwood Flower*. Visit her at www.kathrynstriplingbyer.com.

Joanne M. Clarkson's fourth poetry collection, *Believing the Body*, was published spring 2014 by Gribble Press. Her poems have appeared in over 100 magazines and journals internationally. Clarkson has Master's Degrees in English and Library Science, has taught and worked as a professional librarian. After caring for her mother through a long illness, she re-careered as a Registered Nurse specializing in Hospice and Community Nursing.

Carole Cole lives on the Gulf Coast of Florida with her partner and three cats. When not in the classroom teaching writing and literature, she spends as much time outside as possible. After nearly 30 years, she still believes she lives in paradise.

Lori DeSanti is receiving her MFA Degree from Southern Connecticut State University. Her work has appeared in *Mouse Tales*, *East Coast Literary Review*, *Winter Tangerine Review*, *Extract(s)*, *Adanna* and elsewhere. She is the winner of the 2014 William Kloefkorn Award, a 2013 Pushcart Prize Nominee and a 2014 Best of the Net Nominee.

Sara Diane Doyle makes her home in the wilds of Wyoming where she mingles with antelope, prairie dogs, moose and the elusive jackalope. She was the inaugural Poet Laureate of Poetic Asides in 2008, and spreads her love of poetry wherever she goes. Follow her on Twitter @SestinaNia.

Susan J. Erickson's poems appear in *2River View, Crab Creek Review, Museum of Americana, The Fourth River, Cactus Heart, Naugatuck River Review* and in anthologies including *Malala: Poems for Malala Yousafzai.* Susan lives in Bellingham, Washington, where she helped establish the Sue C. Boynton Poetry Walk and Contest.

Joseph Harker is a linguist-poet frittering away his frantic days in the NYC-Philly metropolis. He's been published here and there, in print and online, he currently edits the journal *Assaracus*, and he's working on his first book-length manuscript. Find him on Twitter: @jhpoet.

Fatima Hirsi is from the water. She is an educator in north Texas, teaching poetry in schools, shelters, and community centers. She's appeared in various stage productions across Texas, and can often be found on sidewalks using her typewriter to birth poems for strangers. Find her at http://flowerwords.wordpress.com.

Brie Huling is a yoga teaching poem writer living in Oregon. She recently landed back in the luscious land of her birth after a wild ride of years and years in Brooklyn. Brie writes poems in order to keep the heart beating. She is fueled by green juice. Om shanti.

Donald Illich's work has appeared in such journals as *The Iowa Review, LIT, Nimrod, Passages North, Rattle,* and *Sixth Finch.* He has been nominated four times for the Pushcart Prize and received a scholarship from the Nebraska Summer Writers Conference. His chapbook is *Rocket Children*.

In another life, **De Jackson** might have been a gypsy, or a pirate. In this one, she's a parent of tweens, and a published poet who's been paid in garbanzo beans, author copies, and one time, a whole dollar. De breathes best in words, spilling some daily at http://WhimsyGizmo.wordpress.com.

Sharon Fagan McDermott is a poet, musician, and teacher living in Pittsburgh, PA. She has published three chapbooks of poetry, most recently, *Bitter Acoustic*, the winner of the Jacar Press 2011 chapbook competition, chosen by the poet Betty Adcock. She also received a 2005 PA Council on the Arts grant for poetry.

Bruce W. Niedt is a southern New Jersey poet whose work has appeared in numerous publications, including *Writer's Digest, US 1 Worksheets, Spitball, The Lyric, Lucid Rhythms,* and *Chantarelle's Notebook.* He has been nominated twice for the Pushcart Prize. His latest chapbook is *Twenty-four by Fourteen*, published by Maverick Duck Press.

Alana Sherman, poet and teacher, lives in Woodbourne, NY, with her husband and dogs in an 1834 farmhouse, under constant renovation (sort of like her poems). She belongs to a group of poets who meet once a month to share their work.

Jay Sizemore sold his soul to corporate America. His work has appeared with magazines like *Prick of the Spindle, DASH, Menacing Hedge,* and *Still: The Journal.* He's won zero awards. Currently, he lives in Nashville, TN, home of the death of modern music. His chapbook *Father Figures* is available on Amazon.

Barton Smock lives in Columbus, Ohio, with his wife and four children. His most recent collection of poetry is self-published and calls itself *The Women You Take From Your Brother.* He writes daily at http://kingsoftrain.wordpress.com.

Cameron Steele is a masters candidate in poetry and research assistant at the University of Nebraska-Lincoln. A native of Virginia, she lives in Lincoln where she works as a freelance journalist and columnist for the *Prairie Schooner* literary journal.

Emma Travis is a languages student at Cambridge University, a part-time poet, and an avid collector of stuffed owls. This is zir first appearance in print, but zir writings are forthcoming in several zines and ze also posts poems online at http://fireandragonstonepoetry. tumblr.com.

k weber lives and writes in northern Kentucky. Her website can be viewed at http://midwesternskirt.moonfruit.com and some of her poetry and podcasts live there, too.

Other titles available from
WORDS DANCE PUBLISHING

I EAT CROW + BLUE COLLAR AT BEST
Poetry by Amanda Oaks + Zach Fishel

| $15 | 124 pages | 5.5" x 8.5" | softcover |

Home is where the heart is and both poets' hearts were raised in the Appalachian region of Western Pennsylvania surrounded by coal mines, sawmills, two-bit hotel taverns, farms, churches and cemeteries. These poems take that region by the throat and shake it until it's bloody and then, they breathe it back to life. This book is where you go when you're looking for nostalgia to kick you in the teeth. This is where you go when you're 200 miles away from a town you thought you'd never want to return to but suddenly you're pining for it.

Amanda and Zach grew up 30 miles from each other and met as adults through poetry. Explore both the male and female perspective of what it's like to grow up hemmed in by an area's economic struggle. These poems mine through life, love, longing and death, they're for home and away, and the inner strength that is not deterred by any of those things.

SPLIT BOOK #1

What are Split Books?

Two full-length books from two poets in one + there's a collaborative split between the poets in the middle!

COLLECT THEM ALL!

Other titles available from
WORDS DANCE PUBLISHING

SHAKING THE TREES
Poetry by Azra Tabassum

| $12 | 72 pages | 5.5" x 8.5" | softcover |

ISBN: 978-0692232408

From the very first page *Shaking the Trees* meets you at the edge of the forest, extends a limb & seduces you into taking a walk through the dark & light of connection. Suddenly, like a gunshot in the very-near distance, you find yourself traipsing though a full-blown love story that you can't find your way out of because the story is actually the landscape underneath your feet. It's okay though, you won't get lost— you won't go hungry. Azra shakes every tree along the way so their fruit blankets the ground before you. She picks up pieces & hands them to you but not before she shows you how she can love you so gently it will feel like she's unpeeling you carefully from yourself. She tells you that it isn't about the bite but the warm juice that slips from the lips down chin. She holds your hand when you're trudging through the messier parts, shoes getting stuck in the muck of it all, but you'll keep going with the pulp of the fruit still stuck in-between your teeth, the juice will dry in the crooks of your elbows & in the lines on your palms. You'll taste bittersweet for days.

"I honestly haven't read a collection like this before, or at least I can't remember having read one. My heart was wrecked by Azra. It's like that opening line in Fahrenheit 451 when Bradbury says, "It was a pleasure to burn." It really was a pleasure being wrecked by it."

— **NOURA**
of *NouraReads*

"I wanted to cry and cheer and fuck. I wanted to take the next person I saw and kiss them straight on the lips and say, "Remember this moment for the rest of your life."

— **CHELSEA MILLER**

WHAT WE BURIED
Poetry by Caitlyn Siehl

| $12 | 64 pages | 5.5" x 8.5" | softcover |

ISBN: 978-0615985862

This book is a cemetery of truths buried alive. The light draws you in where you will find Caitlyn there digging. When you get close enough, she'll lean in & whisper, Baby, buried things will surface no matter what, get to them before they get to you first. Her unbounded love will propel you to pick up a shovel & help— even though the only thing you want to do is kiss her lips, kiss her hands, kiss every one of her stretch marks & the fire that is raging in pit of her stomach. She'll see your eyes made of devour & sadness, she'll hug you & say, Baby, if you eat me alive, I will cut my way out of your stomach. Don't let this be your funeral. Teach yourself to navigate the wound.

"It takes a true poet to write of love and desire in a way that manages to surprise and excite. Caitlyn Siehl does this in poem after poem and makes it seem effortless. Her work shines with a richness of language and basks in images that continue to delight and astound with multiple readings. What We Buried is a treasure from cover to cover."

— **WILLIAM TAYLOR JR.**
Author of *An Age of Monsters*

SPARKLEFAT
Poetry by Melissa May

| \$12 | 62 pages | 5.5" x 8.5" | softcover |

SparkleFat is a loud, unapologetic, intentional book of poetry about my body, about your body, about fat bodies and how they move through the world in every bit of their flash and spark and burst. Some of the poems are painful, some are raucous celebrations, some are reminders and love letters and quiet gifts back to the vessel that has traveled me so gracefully - some are a hymnal of yes, but all of them sparkle. All of them don't mind if you look – really. They built their own house of intention, and they draped that shit in lime green sequins. All of them intend to be seen. All of them have no more fucks to give about a world that wants them to be quiet.

"I didn't know how much I needed this book until I found myself, three pages in, ugly crying on the plane next to a concerned looking business man. This book is the most glorious, glittery pink permission slip. It made me want to go on a scavenger hunt for every speck of shame in my body and sing hot, sweaty R&B songs to it. There is no voice more authentic, generous and resounding than Melissa May. From her writing, to her performance, to her role in the community she delivers fierce integrity & staggering passion. From the first time I watched her nervously step to the mic, to the last time she crushed me in a slam, it is has been an honor to watch her astound the poetry slam world and inspire us all to be not just better writers but better people. We need her.

— **LAUREN ZUNIGA**
Author of *The Smell of Good Mud*

"*SparkleFat* is a firework display of un-shame. Melissa May's work celebrates all of the things we have been so long told deserved no streamers. This collection invites every fat body out to the dance and steams up the windows in the backseat of the car afterwards by kissing the spots we thought (or even hoped) no one noticed but are deserving of love just the same as our mouths."

— **RACHEL WILEY**
Author of the forthcoming *Fat Girl Finishing School*

LOVE AND OTHER SMALL WARS

Poetry by Donna-Marie Riley

| $12 | 76 pages | 5.5" x 8.5" | softcover |

ISBN: 978-0615931111

Love and Other Small Wars reminds us that when you come back from combat usually the most fatal of wounds are not visible. Riley's debut collection is an arsenal of deeply personal poems that embody an intensity that is truly impressive yet their hands are tender. She enlists you. She gives you camouflage & a pair of boots so you can stay the course through the minefield of her heart. You will track the lovely flow of her soft yet fierce voice through a jungle of powerful imagery on womanhood, relationships, family, grief, sexuality & love, amidst other matters. Battles with the heart aren't easily won but Riley hits every mark. You'll be relieved that you're on the same side. Much like war, you'll come back from this book changed.

"Riley's work is wise, intense, affecting, and uniquely crafted. This collection illuminates her ability to write with both a gentle hand and a bold spirit. She inspires her readers and creates an indelible need inside of them to consume more of her exceptional poetry. I could read *Love and Other Small Wars* all day long…and I did."

— **APRIL MICHELLE BRATTEN**
editor of *Up the Staircase Quarterly*

"Riley's poems are personal, lyrical and so vibrant they practically leap off the page, which also makes them terrifying at times. A beautiful debut."

— **BIANCA STEWART**

Other titles available from
WORDS DANCE PUBLISHING

LITERARY SEXTS

A Collection of Short & Sexy Love Poems
(Volume 1)

| $12 | 42 pages | 5.5" x 8.5" | softcover |

ISBN: 978-0615959726

Literary Sexts is a modern day anthology of short love poems with subtle erotic undertones edited by Amanda Oaks & Caitlyn Siehl. Hovering around 50 contributors & 124 poems, this book reads is like one long & very intense conversation between two lovers. It's absolutely breathtaking. These are poems that you would text to your lover. Poems that you would slip into a back pocket, suitcase, wallet or purse on the sly. Poems that you would write on slips of paper & stick under your crush's windshield wiper. Poems that you would write on a Post-it note & leave on the bathroom mirror.

HIT #1
ON AMAZON'S
HOT NEW
RELEASE LIST!

"It's like 100+ new ways to make a reader blush. The imagery is so subtle yet completely thrilling..." **NOW I NEED A COLD SHOWER!"**
- K. W.

"**I DEVOURED IT!** I physically wanted to eat these poems. I wanted to wear them on my skin like perfume..."
- A. G.

"I have consumed this in ways that have left my insides looking like strips of velvet fabric... **SO ORGASMIC!"**
- K. B.

"**A MAELSTROM OF EMOTIONS!** I only hope that there is a Volume 2, a Volume 3 and so on because I need more of this!"
- Daniel CZ

Other titles available from
WORDS DANCE PUBLISHING

Unrequited love? We've all been there.

Enter:

WHAT TO DO AFTER SHE SAYS NO
by Kris Ryan.

This skillfully designed 10-part poem explores what it's like to ache for someone. This is the book you buy yourself or a friend when you are going through a breakup or a one-sided crush, it's the perfect balance between aha, humor & heartbreak.

WHAT TO DO AFTER SHE SAYS NO
A Poem by Kris Ryan

$10 | 104 pages | 5" x 8" | softcover | ISBN: 978-0615870045

"*What to Do After She Says No* takes us from Shanghai to the interior of a refrigerator, but mostly dwells inside the injured human heart, exploring the aftermath of emotional betrayal. This poem is a compact blast of brutality, with such instructions as "Climb onto the roof and jump off. If you break your leg, you are awake. If you land without injury, pinch and twist at your arm until you wake up." Ryan's use of the imperative often leads us to a reality where pain is the only outcome, but this piece is not without tenderness, and certainly not without play, with sounds and images ricocheting off each other throughout. Anticipate the poetry you wish you knew about during your last bad breakup; this poem offers a first "foothold to climb out" from that universal experience."

— **LISA MANGINI**

"Reading Kris Ryan's *What To Do After She Says No* is like watching your heart pound outside of your chest. Both an unsettling visual experience and a hurricane of sadness and rebirth—this book demands more than just your attention, it takes a little bit of your soul, and in the end, makes everything feel whole again."

— **JOHN DORSEY**
author of *Tombstone Factory*

"*What to Do After She Says No* is exquisite. Truly, perfectly exquisite. It pulls you in on a familiar and wild ride of a heart blown open and a mind twisting in an effort to figure it all out. It's raw and vibrant...and in the same breath comforting. I want to crawl inside this book and live in a world where heartache is expressed so magnificently.

— **JO ANNA ROTHMAN**
MA, Coach & Conjurer of Electric Creative Wholeness

Tammy Foster Brewer is the type of poet who makes me wish I could write poetry instead of novels. From motherhood to love to work, Tammy's poems highlight the extraordinary in the ordinary and leave the reader wondering how he did not notice what was underneath all along. I first heard Tammy read 'The Problem is with Semantics' months ago, and it's stayed with me ever since. Now that I've read the entire collection, I only hope I can make room to keep every one of her poems in my heart and mind tomorrow and beyond.

— NICOLE ROSS, author

NO GLASS ALLOWED
Poetry by Tammy Foster Brewer

$12 | 56 pages | 6" x 9" | softcover | ISBN: 978-0615870007

Brewer's collection is filled with uncanny details that readers will wear like the accessories of womanhood. Fishing the Chattahoochee, sideways trees, pollen on a car, white dresses and breast milk, and so much more -- all parts of a deeply intellectual pondering of what is often painful and human regarding the other halves of mothers and daughters, husbands and wives, lovers and lost lovers, children and parents.

— NICHOLAS BELARDES
author of *Songs of the Glue Machines*

Tammy deftly juxtaposes distinct imagery with stories that seem to collide in her brilliant poetic mind. Stories of transmissions and trees and the words we utter, or don't. Of floods and forgiveness, conversations and car lanes, bread and beginnings, awe and expectations, desire and leaps of faith that leave one breathless, and renewed.

"When I say I am a poet / I mean my house has many windows" has to be one of the best descriptions of what it's like to be a contemporary female poet who not only holds down a day job and raises a family, but whose mind and heart regularly file away fleeting images and ideas that might later be woven into something permanent, and perhaps even beautiful. This ability is not easily acquired. It takes effort, and time, and the type of determination only some writers, like Tammy, possess and are willing to actively exercise.

— KAREN DEGROOT CARTER
author of *One Sister's Song*

WORDS DANCE PUBLISHING has one aim:

To spread mind-blowing / heart-opening poetry.

Words Dance artfully & carefully wrangles words that were born to dance wildly in the heart-mind matrix. Rich, edgy, raw, emotionally-charged energy balled up & waiting to whip your eyes wild; we rally together words that were written to make your heart go boom right before they slay your mind. We like Poems that sneak up on you. Poems that make out with you. Poems that bloody your mouth just to kiss it clean. Poems that bite your cheek so you spend all day tonguing the wound. Poems that vandalize your heart. Poems that act like a tin can phone connecting you to your childhood. Fire Alarm Poems. Glitterbomb Poems. Jailbreak Poems. Poems that could marry the land or the sea; that are both the hero & the villain. Poems that are the matches when there is a city-wide power outage. Poems that throw you overboard just dive in & save your ass. Poems that push you down on the stoop in front of history's door screaming at you to knock. Poems that are soft enough to fall asleep on. Poems that will still be clinging to the walls inside of your bones on your 90th birthday. We like poems. Submit yours.

Words Dance Publishing is an independent press out of Pennsylvania. We work closely & collaboratively with all of our writers to ensure that their words continue to breathe in a sound & stunning home. Most importantly though, we leave the windows in these homes unlocked so you, the reader, can crawl in & throw one fuck of a house party.

To learn more about our books, authors, events & Words Dance Poetry Magazine, visit:

WORDSDANCE.COM